IF YOU WANT TO LIVE A HAPPY LIFE, TIE IT TO A GOAL NOT TO PEOPLE OR THINGS

Albert Einstein